MW01002013

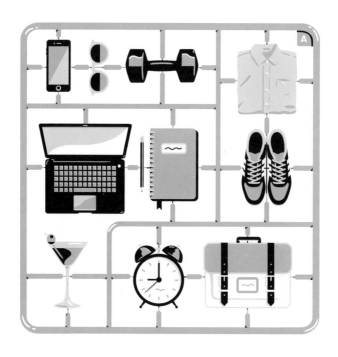

I want to be organised

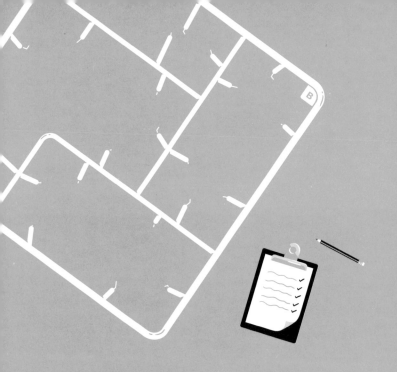

*For Anita - who has helped
keep me organised for the last
20 years. Thank you.*

Other books in the *I want to...* series:

I want to sleep
I want to be calm

I want to be organised

HOW TO DE-CLUTTER YOUR LIFE, MANAGE YOUR TIME
AND GET THINGS DONE

—————— BY ——————

Harriet Griffey

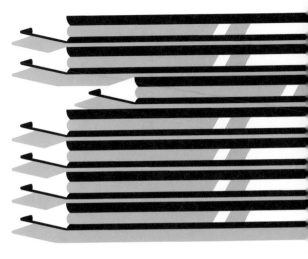

Contents

Why organise?

If you are reading this book it may be that you, or someone you know, would like to be more organised. It may be that you feel life would be simpler and less stressful if you *were* more organised.

It may also come as a surprise that even the most disorganised amongst us can learn to be more organised. What starts out as an effort can become a habit and then a way of life.

> **Unless we begin with the right attitude, we will never find the right solution.** *Chinese proverb*

The benefits of being organised

Have you ever stopped and asked yourself how you can benefit from being organised – why getting rid of clutter and managing your time better might be advantageous to your health and happiness? Here's a quick reminder:

› You'll save time, because many lost minutes spent looking for things add up to lost hours, and that doesn't include the frustration, irritation and stress that can occur when you're in a hurry and can't find your keys or a child's lunch box.

› You'll achieve more, because better organisation enables you to eliminate unnecessary time-wasting, delegate effectively and streamline tasks.

› This, in turn, will give you more time for yourself, to do the things you want to do: exercise, cook more healthily, read the newspaper – and also more time for your family and friends.

› You'll look more professional at work and give a better impression of yourself if you aren't scrabbling around for a misplaced file or being late for appointments.

› You'll save money if you know what you already have and can find it, before you buy more.

› You'll be a better role model – to the team you lead at work, or the team you lead at home. In particular, if you have children, and want them to be well organised and tidy, it will be hard to instil this behaviour unless you apply it yourself. Teaching kids basic organisational skills will be of value for life, while also alleviating the pressure on you to 'do it all' for family members.

› You'll feel better in a calm, well-organised environment. A clutter-free life is automatically more soothing.

Men acquire a particular quality by constantly acting in a particular way... you become just by performing just actions, temperate by performing temperate actions, brave by performing brave actions. *Aristotle*

For many people, the tendency to be organised doesn't come naturally. Time and time again they resolve to get organised, but inevitably fall back into a pattern of disorder and clutter. This is where the creation of a variety of simple systems can bring rewards, and these systems can be easily implemented. Often it's a case of taking regular, simple steps that make a daily difference. Creating a habit of organisation, if you will.

SIMPL

ICITY

is the ultimate sophistication.

LEONARDO DA VINCI

Your organisational personality & style

Are you someone who likes structure in your life, where there is a place for everything, and everything in its place? Or are you happiest when you muddle through, relying on spontaneity and making it up as you go along?

It's seldom as cut and dried as these two extremes suggest, but it is worth having a think about how you respond to clutter and chaos in your external environment, what you find tolerable and what makes you feel uneasy.

Knowing your individual, personal organisational style can be helpful in creating a harmonious setting in which to live and work, or in identifying areas for improvement. It can also be helpful in understanding personality clashes when organisational styles differ, and how to manage those relationships.

Quiz

Try this quick quiz to see how your personality style might affect your organisational profile and then, if you need to, take a look at what steps you could take to improve things.

› **What do you have in your purse/wallet?**

A A debit and credit card; crisp notes; no coins.

B Five different bank cards; two store cards; a handful of notes; lots of loose change.

C Three different bank cards; five store cards; no notes or change; photos of children dating back 20 years; ticket stubs kept from a first date; a pressed flower.

D Can't find my wallet – will look for it later.

› **Before you start work do you:**

A Sit down for five minutes, sort out what's needed, make a list.

B Spend an hour tidying up. You can't work if things are messy.

C Make a cup of coffee, check emails, check phone messages and then start work.

D Spend 30 seconds moving everything off your desk or workspace on to the floor.

› **Do you return personal phone calls:**

A Immediately.

B Within a few hours.

C The next day.

D Forget all about it, until they call back.

› **When working on something, do you:**

A Note the deadline, make a checklist, plan each section.

B Work methodically but get hung up on minor details.

C Underestimate how long the task will take and end up working through the night to stay on schedule.

D Have to extend the deadline at the last minute.

> **When you make an arrangement to meet a friend, do you:**

A Turn up a few minutes early and find a good seat.

B Turn up late, but text beforehand.

C Turn up late – everyone knows you're relaxed about timekeeping.

D What arrangement?

> **What motivates you?**

A Getting it done – when something needs doing, just doing it.

B Promise of a reward at the end – even if that's just five minutes' break on Facebook or a cup of coffee.

C Working in a team, someone telling me what to do next.

D An overdue deadline; I need the adrenaline of anxiety to fuel me.

> **How do you pay your bills?**

A Automatically, via direct debit.

B When I've got several, to do together.

C When I find them buried in a pile, usually at the last minute.

D Often late, incurring penalties.

> **How do you organise your work day?**

A Online calendar with reminders, synchronised with my smartphone.

B It's written down in my diary, and on my smartphone, and on a wall planner.

C It's in my diary – if I can find it…

D I don't. Things just happen.

> **When you leave the house, do you:**

A Make a quick mental check – keys, bag, phone – as you leave.

B Dither on the doorstep mentally checking you've switched off the oven, locked the back door, etc.

C Go back at least once to collect something you've forgotten.

D Lock yourself out so regularly you've had to leave spare keys with a neighbour.

Method-man (or woman!)

The Blitzer

MOSTLY As

Keeps on top of things, all the time. Books are alphabetical; recycling is in the correct bin the moment it's finished with; nothing that is not immediately relevant is kept.

Downside: can be a bit ruthless and unsentimental.

MOSTLY Bs

Everything tends to pile up before having a complete blitz, sorting out and throwing out clutter, although it doesn't tend to stay neat and tidy for that long.

Downside: can get overwhelmed and demotivated halfway through a blitz, and has a tendency to throw the proverbial baby out with the bathwater.

Faux-organised

Chaos-junkie

MOSTLY Cs

Looks fairly organised, but in fact the neat piles have no rhyme or reason. Hangs on to stuff that needs to be recycled, or thrown away, 'in case it comes in useful', or for sentimental reasons.

Downside: easily distracted by looking for things that have got 'buried'.

MOSTLY Ds

Creative appearance and tends to thrive in disorderly surroundings with no appearance of organisation at all and relies on 'remembering' where things are, which isn't infallible.

Downside: tendency to be oblivious to surroundings and a bit unreliable, which can drive family and friends mad.

A place

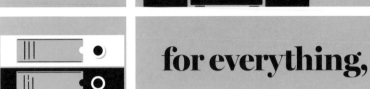

for everything,

and everything

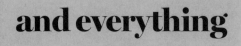

in its

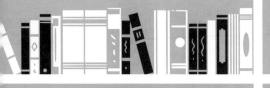

place.

MRS BEETON

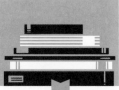

Chaos theory: what stops you getting organised

To the organised, the unorganised person is a mystery. There seems to be no purpose served by not being organised, but this is to ignore some of the underlying psychological reasons as to why chaos can sometimes feel like the better option.

For some, the physical obstacles created by piles of books, stacks of unfiled documents, or laundry baskets full of clothes waiting for attention serve to create a shield against the outside world. These barricades of clutter can be useful in preserving personal boundaries, preventing others getting too close – both literally and metaphorically.

Living in chaos is exhausting, frightening. The catch is that it's also very addictive.

LORNA LUFT, AMERICAN SINGER & ACTRESS, & DAUGHTER OF JUDY GARLAND

For others, being surrounded by 'stuff' is reassuring at a more fundamental level: it makes us feel safe. Having lots of possessions – and 'stocking up' with a surplus of things, from cans of beans to new pens – creates a sense of security, counteracting a feeling of anxiety about not having enough.

Some people find chaos a useful distraction from getting on with the job at hand. It can be a form of procrastination, helping avoid tasks you need to complete or issues you need to address, whether physical or psychological. In the middle of emotional chaos it's sometimes easier to distract ourselves with a scattergun approach to what needs doing.

While some can have a resolutely unsentimental attitude towards possessions, for others the stuff around us represents a time past, a moment lost or some part of ourselves that we wish to cling on to. Because of this, it's tempting to keep these possessions in view, fearing that if they are out of sight, they – and that part of us they represent – will be out of mind.

The downside of this is that we can end up living surrounded by clutter, which can make life even more chaotic. If it begins to feel irritating or overwhelming, then this is an indication that bringing order to chaos is what's needed.

Clutter is stuck energy. The word clutter comes from the Middle English word *clotter*, which means to coagulate – and that's about as stuck as you can get. *Karen Kingston*

We adore chaos because we

love to produce order

M. C. ESCHER

Can't decide?

Decision-making is another area where we can struggle, especially when it comes to getting rid of possessions no longer needed. It can put us off doing something as simple as clearing out a chest of drawers or choosing which clothes to pass on to a charity shop.

Often, simple indecision is the reason that we put off organising or de-cluttering our homes. It can be helpful to keep the organisation you are trying to achieve in mind and use the following quick questions to help make it simpler to decide whether to keep, store or discard something.

> Do you use it regularly?
> Does it work properly, or is it broken?
> Do you find it ugly or uncomfortable?
> Do you actually need more than one?
> Was it a gift you have no use for?
> Are you keeping it, *just in case*?

It helps, too, to be realistic. For example:

> If you haven't worn something for two years because it no longer fits, or you no longer like it, then sell it or take it to a charity shop.
> If you have three potato peelers, but only one that you actually use – at least get rid of one of them!
> If you have read that paperback, recycle it or pass it on. Ditto if it's sat on your shelf for three years without being read, pass it on!
> If you are keeping anything *just in case* it comes in useful, and it hasn't in six months, then it's time to discard it.

Work is a way of bringing order to chaos, and there's a basic satisfaction in seeing that we are able to make something a little more coherent by the end of the day.

ALAIN DE BOTTON, PHILOSOPHER & WRITER

Reduce, reuse, recycle – less stuff, more organised

Less is more, right? But what does this actually mean?

For a start, if you have fewer possessions, you have more time, because you have less to clear up, store or find. Reducing the amount of clutter in your life immediately pays dividends in terms of having more space and fewer chores. Clutter also makes things difficult to find and can be visually overstimulating, creating feelings of stress rather than calm.

As I found I made physical space I had more mental space to question what I was doing with my time – the most precious commodity I had. *Chris Wray, minimalist lifestyle blogger*

Clutter is the physical manifestation of unmade decisions fuelled by procrastination. *Christina Scalise*

Clutter

A University of California, Los Angeles, study on contemporary suburban American lives in 2005 revealed that people owned a staggering number of possessions: stored, hoarded and stockpiled. What they also discovered was that all these possessions actually created stress, especially for the mothers of the families, who frequently used words like 'mess' and 'very chaotic' and 'not fun' to describe their homes, and this was borne out by the levels of the stress hormone cortisol found in saliva tests.

Reduce

› Start by reducing the amount of stuff you buy and you will automatically reduce the amount of possessions you need to find homes for.

› When shopping, try to differentiate between need and want. To need something means it's essential; and while it's valid to want something too, this must be because you will use it or get pleasure from it.

› Avoid buying more than you planned – *buy one get one free* offers are only a saving if you needed the item in the first place (plus a spare).

› If you shop online for your groceries, be wary of over-buying. It's difficult to plan a whole week's worth of food in advance, which may explain why we waste and throw away so much. A better option may be to buy household essentials like toilet paper, washing powder and store cupboard basics online, giving you more freedom to plan daily meals based on what you feel like eating that day, for which you can buy locally.

› When present-buying, think about shared experiences as a gift – organise a theatre outing, perhaps, or cook a delicious meal – rather than adding to the clutter by making a haphazard guess at something your loved one might like, just because you feel you ought to give them something.

A house is just a pile of stuff with a cover on it.

GEORGE CARLIN, AMERICAN COMEDIAN & SOCIAL CRITIC

CLOTHES SHOPPING CHECKLIST

- If you need to update your wardrobe, spend some time thinking about how the new garment will fit with the rest of your clothes and what basic style, colour and look you are aiming for.

- Set your budget. Stick to it unless you can guarantee a cost-per-wear ratio that justifies the price, and then the old adage 'you only regret your economies, not your extravagances' may apply!

- Look in magazines and online for ideas about styles, prices and where to shop.

- Allow enough time for shopping – and take a break during the process. Too little time can result in impulse buying.

- Go with a friend only if you feel it will improve or enhance the process and you value their judgement about what is right for you.

- Take with you any garment or accessory that needs to match the item you are shopping for.

- Always keep your receipt in case you need to return an item. And make sure you know the store's returns policy, as the time allowed tends to vary.

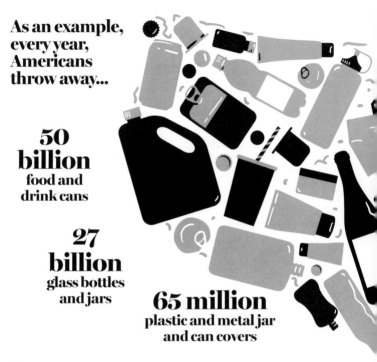

As an example, every year, Americans throw away...

50 billion
food and drink cans

27 billion
glass bottles and jars

65 million
plastic and metal jar and can covers

Reuse

The success of online marketing places like eBay and Gumtree, and of specialist websites like musicMagpie, is testament to the possibilities of de-cluttering. If you don't want it, someone else might, and there are plenty of opportunities to pass on unwanted stuff – via charity shops or to earn money.

When it comes to unwanted presents, re-gifting is allowed, but be careful not to hurt someone's feelings by giving away something they valued when they gave it to you.

30%+
of waste is packaging
materials

85%
of garbage is sent to
a dump, or landfill,
where it can take
from 100 to 400 years
for things like cloth
and aluminium to
decompose. Glass has
been found in perfect
condition after 4,000
years in the earth!

WWW.FACTMONSTER.COM

Recycle

From glass, plastics, clothing and paper to composting, batteries and
electronic items, recycling items in an effort to reduce pollution via landfill
sites has to be done. Nearly everything can be recycled now – printer ink
cartridges, mobile phones, spectacles, video tapes and even old bras – a
quick online search will enable you to see what's possible and in your area.
Not only will you feel better for getting rid of something you no longer use,
like, want, or have space for, but you also get to feel good about doing your
bit for the planet.

The joy of lists

Some people are natural list-makers; some are not.

If you despise the idea of making lists but are struggling to save time and be more organised, you may want to revisit this idea. List-making is a very simple way of organising ourselves, because the very act of making a list demands that we stop, think and plan in logical sequence the most effective way to get things done, while writing stuff down helps the mind to focus.

Human beings love lists, because they create a sense of order in a chaotic world. *Shaun Usher,* Lists of Note

We create lists of places we want to visit, books we want to read, food we need to buy, tasks we need to complete and ideas we want to remember.

There is a positive psychology attached to all this. Making a list is often a first step towards committing to the task; it clarifies thinking and makes whatever needs to be done look more manageable. It also relieves the stress of trying to remember everything; written down, your organised thoughts function as a checklist. You feel in control because the details are committed to paper, and being able to cross things off when they're done promotes feelings of satisfaction.

> **The list is the origin of culture. It's part of the history of art and literature. What does culture want? To make infinity comprehensible... And how, as a human being, does one face infinity? How does one grasp the incomprehensible? Through lists...**
>
> *Umberto Eco, philosopher & novelist*

The science bit

List-making also helps counteract something called the Zeigarnik Effect, named after Bluma Zeigarnik, a Soviet psychologist who noticed that waiters in a busy restaurant in 1920s Vienna had a better recollection of those orders still unpaid than those paid – but only until the task was completed. Once an order was paid, they forgot it instantly.

Zeigarnik designed a series of experiments to work out why incomplete tasks stick in the memory, publishing her research in 1927. It would seem that we all like to finish what we start; if we don't, it niggles away at us. Because of this, we carry details of unfinished tasks in our heads until they are completed – a bit like having a file constantly open on your computer, slowing everything down. Writing a list frees us up by removing unfinished business from our working memory, where it is lodged for fear of being forgotten, and filing it away in a safe place for retrieval.

Cooking up a list

One of the simplest examples of a good list is a cooking recipe. First it presents you with a list of ingredients to check off before you start, then it lists the process of what needs to be done in the correct order to fulfil the goal.

That same principle can be applied to the kind of lists you make every day. Take food shopping, for example. Writing items down as you remember them – in the Notes function of your smartphone or on the back of an envelope – is a helpful start. Grouping the items you need acts as a memory prompt; plus, when it comes to supermarket shopping, for example, similar items are located in the same aisle, so this also saves time. What's more, if it's a supermarket where you shop regularly, you can list items in the order in which you make your way around the store.

So your list may begin to look something like this:

› Potatoes	› Butter	› Bin bags
› Onions	› Yoghurt	› Toilet paper
› Carrots	› Minced beef	› Toothpaste
› Apples	› Sausages	› Etc. etc.
› Milk	› Washing-up liquid	

And you can hope to end up at the till with all you meant to buy: no more and no less!

Lists and creativity

Lists can also help with creativity – and can be transformed into mind maps, so beloved of brainstorming sessions. Again, committing these to paper creates a tangible record and resource, which can be referred to at a later stage. No wonder so many writers and creatives carry a notebook and pen with them at all times. Making lists of words and ideas can be a first step towards the creative process of writing.

These lists were the provocations, finally, that caused my better stuff to surface. I was feeling my way toward something honest, hidden under the trapdoor on the top of my skull.

RAY BRADBURY, AUTHOR OF
FAHRENHEIT 451

The benefits of routine

Benjamin Franklin, one of the founding fathers of the United States, was very big on routine and organisation. Ever wondered who said, 'Early to bed and early to rise makes a man healthy, wealthy and wise'? That was Benjamin Franklin, a great list-maker who devised a daily routine to live by that included rising at 5 a.m. and going to sleep at 1 a.m. (presumably with some nap time in between!). In order to thrive in a world that tends towards chaos, Franklin compiled his first list, of 13 virtues, at the age of 20. 'Let all your things have their places,' he wrote. 'Let each part of your business have its time.'

A schedule defends from chaos and whim.
Annie Dillard, American writer

Daily routines

Daily routines tend to fall into two categories: personal and work-related. On the mornings and evenings of a working day, the priority is to have a personal routine that becomes a habit. This can help create space in the day for what you want to do.

Routines are the ideal way to bookend your day. I think they are the building blocks of effectiveness, efficiency and efficacy.

MIKE VARDY, PRODUCTIVITY EXPERT

Evening routine

Because what you do before you go to bed can have an impact on how smoothly the next day begins, it makes sense to start with an evening routine.

› Check your diary for the following day.
› Work out what you need – keys, travel pass, work folder, sports kit, etc. – and leave these ready.
› Select the clothes you want to wear and ensure shoes are cleaned and shirts are ironed (if you prefer to do this in the morning, allow enough time).
› Get into the habit of washing up or putting the dishwasher on, throwing any rubbish away and straightening your living room before bed – it makes the start of the day feel easier!

Morning routine

A morning routine takes away the need to think about what you have to do to get out of the door on time – giving your brain time to catch up with your body in the morning.

› Your first step is to determine when you need to leave home to be sure of arriving at your destination on time. Work backwards from that.
› Get up early enough to do what you want to do – e.g. take a shower, eat breakfast, exercise – before you leave. For some of us, 10 minutes is all we need to prepare for the day, but others need more, so be realistic.
› Factor in 10 minutes' contingency for those unexpected things that can come up and delay you. If they don't, then you have the advantage of a bit of leeway.

This takes roughly 51 minutes, so if you have to leave the house at 8 a.m. to be sure of reaching your destination on time, the alarm needs to go off at 7 a.m.

Nobody can go back and start a new beginning, but anyone can start today and make a new ending.

Maria Robinson, child development expert

Don't fear routine

Rather than stifling creativity, an effective and time-efficient routine gives us more time to 'stand and stare', and simply enjoy life. In addition, with a routine in place, essential tasks can be achieved without much thought, freeing up the mind to wander and wonder.

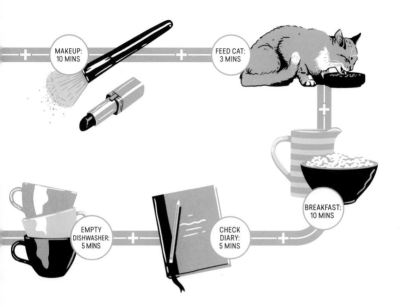

The reality is that many a creative soul has thrived on routine. Working in a bank didn't stop T. S. Eliot's creativity; and whatever time he'd been drinking until the night before, Ernest Hemingway habitually rose around 5.30 a.m. to start work. Just like these 20th-century heavyweights, once you've realised the benefits of routine, you may never go back.

Routines remove the need to deliberate over what you should do when (which takes time and energy), because once you've established a routine you've already made those decisions. *Heidi Grant Halvorson, social psychologist*

Organise your family

Organising yourself is one thing; organising others is a learnt skill, not least because you have to accommodate other people's organisational types.

Living alongside someone who has a different organisational style to your own can be tricky. And then there are families. Within which, the organisational mix can be exasperatingly diverse!

A family is a place where principles are hammered and honed on the anvil of everyday living.

Charles R. Swindoll, Christian pastor

Your family may consist of you and the cat – for now. Or you and a partner. Or you, a partner and six children – several of whom are not your own. Inevitably, though, the general day-to-day organisation tends to fall into one person's lap.

That person may be you. And while you may welcome that responsibility, it's worth thinking about what can be usefully delegated, shared or ignored, negotiated with a partner, or instigated as children grow up. If you want to organise the sort of family involvement that helps general organisation and teaches life skills to offspring, it's as well to start early and catch them while they're young.

Family philosophy

Unless you want to end up doing everything yourself, instil the family philosophy that you work together *as a team*. This way, it's not *your job* that the washing-up needs doing, it's just something that has to be done – an important point when someone asks if you need any help. Without making a heavy-handed point, the answer to offers of 'help' is to say, 'Yes – the washing-up needs doing and it would be good if you would do it. Thank you.'

You may be the family's CEO but that doesn't mean their contribution is less valid than yours and washing-up is just one of many jobs that need doing to keep Team Family functioning. Thinking about it like this can also take some of the heat out of a situation, because it's not about one person's or another's job – it's just something that needs doing.

Prioritise

Decide what is essential to you and your family; useful; an optional extra; or simply a case of life's too short:

› **Essential:** getting to school on time, clean underwear, the recycling...
› **Useful:** cleaning the bath after every use, bulk buying toilet paper, milk delivery...
› **Optional extra:** sorting out the sock drawer, polishing furniture, flower arranging...

› **Life's too short:** bread-making, window cleaning (pay someone else), ironing sheets...

This list of priorities will be completely personal to you. If, for example, one person actively likes bread-making, or polishing furniture, then that can become part of their contribution to family life.

Meals

In an ideal world, the opportunity to share a meal lies at the heart of family life. In reality, our busy lifestyles and a variety of home/work/school/social life clashes mean that family meals can become complicated and stressful.

Without being completely inflexible, instigating regular mealtimes, from which a deviation is the exception rather than the norm, can help family harmony. Of course, food as sustenance is important, but sharing a family meal together also provides a regular, unforced opportunity to communicate and share important as well as more trivial family news, ideas and aspirations.

Time...

The other major issue in family organisation is time. Everyone has demands on their time – from work meetings to parents' evenings to swimming classes – which need organising.

A family wall planner or calendar can be a great resource here and should be updated regularly. Individuals can be colour-coded for easier reference – and a note made if the activity of one requires the involvement of another. For example, if a parent is needed to drive a child to a location.

In addition, a regular diary catch-up for busy families – once a week over dinner – can provide an opportunity to share details and agree plans. It also encourages children to participate in family arrangements, make decisions and start to take responsibility for what they may need to contribute or do.

The family is the country of the heart.

Giuseppe Mazzini, Italian revolutionary

Children have never been very good at listening to their elders, but they have never failed to imitate them.

JAMES BALDWIN, AMERICAN WRITER & SOCIAL CRITIC

Young children

At what age can a child start to contribute to the organisation of family life? Again, this can differ from family to family, but even a toddler can help pick up their toys at the end of a play session. In fact, picking up toys can almost be as much of a game as the game itself. Make it easy by having a box or basket in which books, soft toys, building blocks and so on can be easily stored. (If you colour-code the containers, you can extend the 'game' by inviting your toddler to allocate the toys by type.) And always instigate 'five minutes' tidy-up' before the end of play, to create the habit of tidying up, even from a young age.

Never underestimate the example you set your children: they will always take their cue from you.

A note on teenagers' brains

Ever wondered why your teenager is so hopelessly disorganised? It's because of a massive developmental change in the brain, particularly in the frontal cortex – the area responsible for executive planning, the ability to keep more than one thought in mind, planning future tasks, focusing attention, controlling impulsive behaviour and, generally, being able to organise themselves.

It will benefit them (and you!) if you suggest simple strategies to help with losing keys/missing buses/timetabling schoolwork/managing time, almost as if they were – frustratingly – much younger. It's a maturation process that takes longer in some than others, and it's also an opportunity to start learning to become self-reliant, which will serve them well in adult life.

Home improvements

Have nothing in your house that you do not know to be useful or believe to be beautiful. *William Morris*

Morris may well have been on to something when it comes to helping us to keep our homes well organised and tidy. He cited two qualities – usefulness and beauty – to help us identify what possessions are of value to us, or necessary to our daily lives.

The potato peeler example

The notion of what is essential can change but – whichever way you look at it – you don't need two of the same essential item. So, if you have one potato peeler that you use and like, is there much point in having two – or three, or four? Or, if you never peel potatoes, there's no reason to have one at all. Following this logic, it becomes much easier to remove inessential items from your home, de-cluttering possessions and clearing the way towards a less stressful existence.

Making a start

It's too easy to become distracted by sentimental attachment, memories and associations. To avoid being overwhelmed by indecision, one of the best ways to start de-cluttering and reorganising your home is to tackle belongings by subject – clothes, books, crockery, and so on. This makes decision-making easier, and also helps with the processing of what comes next. For example, when sorting books – which may yield six books or six cartons of books to be got rid of – dealing with them all at once immediately means you can draw a line under *Books: Sorted*, and move on to your next subject area – clothes, for example.

Start by selecting those items that you *definitely* want to keep (which have passed the criteria on page 26) before gathering the rest to be donated to charity shops, recycled or thrown away.

Some aspects of organising our home depend on what we do there. For example, if we work from home we need to create space for any materials or items related to the work we do, and organise these. We may have a separate room, or need to create room within our living space.

What the mind can conceive, the mind can achieve.

W. CLEMENT STONE

Organise your kitchen

Whether you have a small galley kitchen or a huge kitchen-dining room, the principles of this room's use remain the same: here is where you store, prepare and cook the meals you eat, and clean and wash up afterwards. So a kitchen's primary function is to fulfil that role.

When it comes to basic organisation in a kitchen, you need easy-to-clean surfaces, space to work and room to store kitchen equipment and utensils when not in use. The other requirement for a kitchen, of all the rooms in your home, is that it should be safe – not just in terms of food hygiene, but also for personal safety as you will be storing and working with sharp implements and also hot, sometimes boiling, substances. A disorganised kitchen can lead to accidents – burns, scalds, cuts and slips on spills – making the kitchen potentially the most dangerous room in your home!

The layout of your kitchen will also help in your organisation and you can break this down into six main areas, which inevitably have to interact harmoniously with each other:

1. Food storage
2. Food preparation
3. Equipment and utensils storage
4. Cooking facilities
5. Sink and water supply
6. Garbage (which may include composting and recycling)

Food storage areas

These will include your fridge, a pantry for those fortunate enough, but more usually a cupboard or series of cupboards for dry, tinned or bottled supplies.

Group similar cooking ingredients together: so on one shelf you may have all your pasta, rice, noodles and so on, and on another, stock cubes, dried herbs, spices, salt and pepper. If you don't cook at home very often, you may find that you only need limited stores.

Your fridge is best kept for those foods that deteriorate quickly – milk, meat, salad vegetables, etc. Regularly check and clear any items past their use-by or best-before dates, and keep an eye on how long you have kept food in the freezer.

Saving time

If you like to cook, make additional quantities that can be frozen for quick ready meals during the working week, rather than buying shop-bought convenience food. Sauces for pasta, meat casseroles and curries can be enjoyed on the day of cooking, then the surplus frozen, and defrosted and reheated at a later date.

Food preparation area

Ideally this should be between your cooking area and water supply. In a small kitchen this isn't difficult, but if your kitchen is large it might need to be reorganised to make best use of space.

Storage

It isn't hard to accumulate a variety of pots and pans, basic or specialised, depending on your cooking skills and inclinations. Some of these you will use every day and others only occasionally.

Those items – pan/bowl/knife/board – you use every day should be immediately accessible, either in a cupboard close to the food preparation or cooking area, or hanging from a bar on the wall or overhead, depending on your kitchen design. More specialised equipment – the pasta maker, vegetable spiralizer, ice-cream maker, and so on – can be stored in less accessible spaces. (Better still, if you've only ever used these items twice in as many years, get rid of them!)

There is an infinite range of storage possibilities for food items – from plastic, airtight boxes to trays. Similarly, there are ingenious ways to make better use of space in your kitchen, especially if this is at a premium for you. For example, if your shelving is too widely spaced, there are shelf organisers, over-door storage racks, plate racks, stacking caddies and so on, to help pack more into your space.

Store delicate glassware separately from crockery, and don't put heavy items high up or low down, but ideally just above or below waist height.

If you have a dining room, you can allocate a couple of drawers here for mealtime cutlery, tablecloths, mats, napkins, crockery and glassware – that way they'll be closer to the table at which you sit to eat.

If you don't make cookies, you don't need 20 cookie cutters.

THE MINIMALISTS, JOSHUA FIELDS MILLBURN & RYAN NICODEMUS

Cooking area

Ideally, the surfaces either side of your oven and hob are heat resistant, so that you can move something hot from the oven or hob and put it down without damaging your work surface. If this isn't the case, you will need to add a heat-resistant board to your kitchen equipment.

Garbage disposal

If there is space, this can be built in, usually under the sink. If the garbage disposal and recycling bins need to be freestanding, find a space as close to the sink as possible. Proximity to your cleaning area makes it easy to regularly disinfect.

Regular tasks to keep your kitchen organised

It may be that you do most of this regularly to stay organised – if not, use these suggestions to help organise your kitchen more efficiently.

Once a day: Wash up and wipe all surfaces clean. If you keep pets, you may want to use an antibacterial cleaner; otherwise hot, soapy water is sufficient for most germs.

Rinse and wring out dishcloths – avoid leaving them in a sopping wet heap to harbour germs.

Wipe up any spills on a cooking hob as they happen or at the end of a cooking session, otherwise they can become 'baked' on and more difficult to remove.

Keep chopping boards for vegetables separate from those for meat to avoid cross-contamination. And don't use the same board for chopping onions, garlic or chilli peppers as you do for slicing bread, as it will become tainted in taste. Again, a quick scrub with hot, soapy water then leaving to dry after use, should be sufficient.

Every few days: Wash tea towels at 60°C: they tend to stay damp for a while, providing good breeding grounds for germs. If you dry the cloths in sunshine, the ultraviolet light will kill off any residual bugs.

Once a week: Disinfect cloths, sinks, garbage containers and drains – a solution of water and household bleach (follow instructions on the bottle) is sufficient.

Check the fridge for any out-of-date foods: cooked or uncooked. Wipe fridge shelves and clean the salad drawer with a solution of bicarbonate of soda (baking soda) – one tablespoon to two pints of warm water. Buy it in bulk form
at the chemist's – it's a cheap, safe kitchen cleanser that cuts through grease and helps reduce smells.

If you have a microwave, you can also use this same cleaning technique: put a small cup of bicarbonate of soda solution inside and heat on high for a minute, to allow the steam to do some of the work for you.

Also use bicarbonate of soda to keep drains grease free by pouring a dry cupful down the plughole followed by a little warm water before leaving for an hour.

Once a month: Clean the oven. If you have wiped up spills along the way, this shouldn't be too arduous, but regularly keeping it clean will prevent the sort of build-up that makes it hard to remove. If you don't use the oven much, this may not need doing as regularly – it depends on your lifestyle.

Once every six months: Check that things are in their designated place, reorganise or reallocate space according to what's needed. If you share a kitchen, even if only with family members, things can get put back in the wrong place.

Check out-of-date or nearly out-of-date products and items – make sure you use up what's coming to the end of its shelf life first.

Once a year: Go through utensils and recycle or throw out any items you haven't used for a year, anything broken or duplicated.

Clean inside of cupboards.

Organise your living room

Home is where the heart is. *Anon*

The clue is in the name. Your living room is where you spend a lot of time living your life – socialising with family and friends; watching television; listening to music; relaxing and chilling out. It may also be where you work and eat.

In fact, a living room can be so multipurpose it can become the room in which everything gets dumped. Avoid this by keeping a check on the following:

For a quick five-minute makeover, empty rubbish bins, straighten any cushions or throws, replace books on shelves, discard dying flowers, stack DVDs, throw out newspapers. Get into the habit of doing this before bed and it will help you start your day in a more organised fashion.

Keep seats and sofas clear: don't clutter them up with clothes, coats, papers or books.

Avoid having piles of things on the floor – keep floor space clear. This may mean rethinking rugs or other floor coverings that need constant straightening.

Assess your storage. Maybe adding a simple bookshelf or closet would enable you to keep your living room better organised.

Regularly cull shelves of books, ornaments, photographs, etc. – reduce, reuse, recycle (see pages 29-35) – to keep surfaces clutter free.

Keep a basket in which you can gather up anything that finds its way into the living room that doesn't belong there – shoes, books, children's toys, old newspapers. These can be redistributed, recycled or disposed of once a day.

Habit is habit, and not to be flung out of the window by any man, but coaxed downstairs a step at a time.

MARK TWAIN

Making a small space work better

However large a living room is, by the time there are several family members or visitors using it, it can feel small. Even after you have de-cluttered and redistributed items back to their primary storage space (coats on hooks in the hall, newspapers recycled, crockery in the kitchen, etc.) there are a number of things that can be done to make your living room feel more spacious and better organised.

> Keep background colours pale, and furniture a similar colour, or tones of the same.
> Create one wall of floor-to-ceiling shelving (matching the walls in colour) that can house books, DVDs, framed photographs, precious ornaments.
> Avoid patterned carpets or multiple rugs: consider stripping floorboards and painting them if their quality isn't great.

Organise your bathroom

Keeping your bathroom organised may feel like the equivalent of painting the proverbial Forth Bridge in Scotland – once it's done, it's time to do it all over again. So the main aim in a bathroom is to think about how to streamline those jobs that constantly need doing again and again (and again!) to keep it organised.

Storage

Bathrooms can get overpopulated with products, especially if each family member wants to use different items. You can easily end up with a multitude of shampoos, shower gels, facial scrubs, and so on, that clutter up bathroom surfaces.

› As a general rule, store anything that isn't used on a daily basis, leaving out only those products you use every day.
› Use up items rather than having endless half-empty bottles.
› Regularly cull the products that have expired or you never use, and get rid of unnecessary packaging.

> Use drawer or shelf dividers for beauty products that are smaller in size and can get muddled and damaged if dumped together.
> If space is in short supply, use an over-the-door shoe holder in which you can store items not in everyday use.
> Use over-the-door hooks for hanging dressing gowns and other clothes as you undress.
> Keep a laundry bin in the bathroom – it can be small and double as a seat – so that dirty clothes can be tidied away immediately, rather than being left on the floor.

Towels

Avoid sharing towels, and remember that damp towels will harbour germs and should be washed regularly.

A heated towel rail, or a rack over a radiator for drying and airing damp towels in between use, avoids your having to use a fresh towel every time and reduces environmentally unfriendly washing and drying.

Clean towels can be kept folded in a closet. If you have a hot water tank that keeps the bathroom warm, this is the ideal place for an airing cupboard.

Group towels by size: face cloths, hand towels, bath towels and bath sheets. If you have the space, store each group in individual containers or on separate shelves.

Children's bath toys

If you are blessed with children, bath time can be a fun but damp end to their day, and can leave you sorting out a scummy bath full of bits of plastic. Use a plastic basket in which the wet toys can drain in the bath and which, once emptied, can then be transferred out of the bath, and even out of sight in a cupboard, until the next time. Bath toys can be rotated so that the pile doesn't become too enormous, and regularly culled when they are broken, mildewed or no longer functioning.

Shower storage

Showers without any internal shelving can benefit from having a hanging organiser over the showerhead, or storage containers that use suction pads on the shower walls, to store soap and washing items.

Cleaning

Keep a bottle of bathroom cleaner and a sponge or cloth easily accessible, so that the bath can be cleaned after use, while it's still warm and easier to remove any soap scum. Keep a window or 'squeegee' wiper by the shower, to use on glass shower screens after use. Making a habit of wiping down the shower screen immediately after every use reduces the necessity for heavy-duty cleaning later. Many squeegee wipers are designed to attach to the shower wall with a suction pad for storage.

Lighting

While you need decent light in a bathroom to see what you're doing (when you floss your teeth, for example), having the option to dim the lights for a relaxing bath is worth considering.

Failing that, scented candles and some bath oil, plus maybe a little gentle music, can organise your bathroom into a relaxing personal spa!

Organise your bedroom

We spend around a third of our lives asleep, so the bedroom fulfils an important role. And, because this is where we go to sleep and restore our minds and bodies, it should ideally be a place of calm and relaxation.

If you want to change the world, start off by making your bed.
Admiral William H. McRaven, US naval commander

The bed

Your bedroom may be large, it may be small, it may be shared or it may have to double as a study or workroom, but, primarily, it should be a place of sleep. To that end, your bed will be the focal point of the room – and there is seldom a more delicious or satisfying feeling than when the bed is made up with clean linen, ready to slip into at the end of a busy day. If you have to fight your way into a bed of rumpled bedclothes, tangled sheets and crumpled pillows, strewn with clothes and other junk, it can contribute to feeling at odds with the world, ending your day on a discordant note.

A simple way of bringing an organised feel to your life is to make your bed every day. This is easy and quick to do if you have a duvet or continental quilt. When you get up, simply fold the quilt back to air while you shower and dress, then give it a shake, smooth it straight and plump up the pillows ready for your return.

Immediately the bedroom looks more organised.

If your bed has to double as a couch during the day, keep a bedspread, blanket or cover to throw over it, to keep clean the sheets on which you actually sleep.

Sleep

Sleep can be elusive for some, so organising your bedroom so that it's a place of tranquillity and calm can help. Avoid having a television or computer in the bedroom: it's just too tempting to watch, work or play on before trying to sleep, and the light from the screen is very stimulating, preventing the secretion of the sleep-inducing hormone melatonin. If you read in bed, choose books rather than backlit screen devices for the same reason.

It is a common experience that a problem difficult at night is resolved in the morning after the committee of sleep has worked on it.

JOHN STEINBECK

Cupboards and closets

As the bedroom is usually the place where we dress and start our day, the wardrobe, cupboards or closets that hold our clothes are second in importance to the bed. Keeping them organised will enable us to find things quickly and easily, and stop the bedroom looking like a rummage or jumble sale, with clothes left lying on the floor, bed, chairs or other furniture. It really doesn't take any longer to drop dirty clothes into a laundry basket (either in the bedroom or elsewhere) than it does to drop them on the floor.

Clothes last longer and look better if they are folded or hung up after wearing, but the biggest problem many of us face is that we have too many clothes for our storage space. If this is you, it's time for a clothes cull (see page 26 for tips) – after which, improve the organisation of your closet. Having pared down your wardrobe to those clothes you actually wear, and which are relevant to your daily life, then look to its organisation.

Closet makeover

› Use decent hangers on which you can hang coats, jackets, dresses, blouses and shirts, along with trousers and skirts.
› Find a system to organise your clothes by that works for you, and use it. You may group clothes together by type – for example, all dresses and all shirts together – colour-code, or sort by season.
› If you have separate storage for off-season clothes and shoes, use it – but don't keep anything you haven't worn for over a year.
› Fold and store T-shirts, jumpers and other knitwear on a shelf or in a drawer, rather than on hangers: they take up less space and keep their shape better.
› Keep all underwear in one section, socks in another, for easy access.
› If you have a dresser, or chest of drawers, keep each drawer or section for one group of clothing items.
› Repair and clean clothes, if necessary, before you need to wear them, and keep a small sewing kit in your closet for this purpose (the kind given away free in hotels is fine here).
› Check regularly for moths that can damage natural fabrics: cedar wood moth repellent balls or lavender can help protect woollen garments.

Organise your work life

We spend a lot of time at work, either formally or informally, throughout a lifetime. Few of us have the sort of work that relies solely on ourselves, and most of us have to organise our work life around other people, their demands and structures. This is true whether you're waiting tables, the CEO of a major company, or the intern at a start-up.

Whoever you are and whatever you do, how you do it will impact on others. Also, there may be times when your work/life balance is not as you would like it – and taking a look at how you organise it can help improve things.

Time management

Much of what makes the organisation of your work life better is the way you manage your time. Over the years, many workplace gurus and time-management experts have applied their minds to key facets of organisation that can make the difference, and these can be distilled into 12 key points:

1. Differentiate between what is urgent and what is important. Prioritise these and don't make the mistake of getting bogged down with what is urgent, but not important. Learn to focus on what serves you best in the long run.

2. Set goals. If you don't know what you're aiming to achieve at work, it's difficult to know when you've achieved it! This can include smaller tasks and major accomplishments over a day, week, month or year – you decide what your timescale and deadline are.

3. Don't overcommit. Be realistic about how long it takes to do something and allow enough time, negotiate for a later deadline or say 'no' if you need to.

4. Create realistic deadlines. Allied to the point above, don't be pressurised to commit to a timescale on which you will fail to deliver.

5. Plan your time. We all work in different ways and experience makes this easier, but taking a few moments to actually think through and plan how to organise your time before you start will pay dividends.

6. Allow time for the unexpected: factor in a bit of leeway to allow for unanticipated demands that may crop up.

7. Do things once. For example, rather than read an email and then come back to it, read it once and, if you can, reply straightaway.

8. Develop routines. The benefit of a routine (see page 43-47) is that it reduces the need to think about some of the tasks that you do regularly.

9. Avoid multitasking. Focusing on one thing at a time means you can actually work your way through a task faster. It's a much more efficient and less stressful way of working.

10. Minimise distractions. If you are constantly checking your emails while trying to do a piece of work, it can take time to refocus and will in fact waste your precious time.

11. Delegate. Where you can, outsource or delegate work others can do. This requires you to learn the skill of briefing that person well, so that

Give me six hours to chop down a tree and I will spend the first four sharpening the axe.

ABRAHAM LINCOLN

they deliver what you ask without your constantly having to check up on them. Make sure they know exactly what's expected of them, what they will need in order to execute it and within what timescale. Get them to confirm their understanding of the task – and then don't micromanage, but let them get on with it!

12. Factor in time off from work. The whole purpose of good time management is that you don't spend all your time at work. So include downtime and quieter days in your work schedule. Remember, problem-solving often occurs spontaneously when we take time out.

STEPHEN COVEY, AUTHOR OF *THE 7 HABITS OF HIGHLY EFFECTIVE PEOPLE*, CAME UP WITH THE FOLLOWING:

- Be proactive
- Begin with the end in mind
- Put first things first
- Think win-win
- Seek first to understand, and then to be understood
- Synergise
- Sharpen the saw

Organise your student life

For some students, this new-found independence and life away from the domestic structure of home is a wonderful liberation. For others, staying on top of the day-to-day stuff while getting to grips with term-time schedules, work deadlines, tutorials, assignments and other demands can feel like an impossible challenge.

Relax

Much of organising your student life is simple time management (see pages 85-89) and with the aid of a few basic guidelines it's possible to get organised and stay on top of work commitments without breaking a sweat, while enjoying this unique period of your life, making new friends and having fun.

Your time is limited; so don't waste it living someone else's life.

STEVE JOBS

Organising your work

› Allocate space to study (reserve your bed for sleep!), and blocks of time when you can concentrate without distractions.

› Regularly review, check and update your working schedule – if not daily, then weekly. Use digital services – apps, Google diary, smartphone calendars – to help, and utilise programmed alerts to remind you of important deadlines.

› Learn to prioritise – and tackle first anything that requires thinking time, research or input from others.

› Break down complex tasks into smaller, more manageable chunks that build towards the final outcome.

› Before a tutorial or teaching session, review previous work in preparation. Likewise, after a lecture, check what you might need to do to follow up or reinforce learning.

› Assess what independent learning is required and factor this into your schedule, allowing enough time to complete any preparatory work.

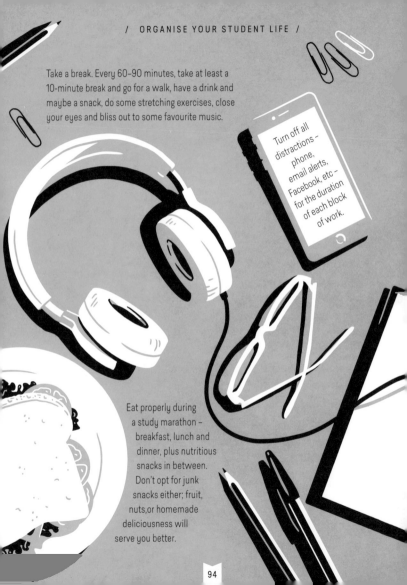

Take a break. Every 60–90 minutes, take at least a 10-minute break and go for a walk, have a drink and maybe a snack, do some stretching exercises, close your eyes and bliss out to some favourite music.

Turn off all distractions – phone, email alerts, Facebook, etc – for the duration of each block of work.

Eat properly during a study marathon – breakfast, lunch and dinner, plus nutritious snacks in between. Don't opt for junk snacks either; fruit, nuts, or homemade deliciousness will serve you better.

Keep hydrated – but opt
for water, fruit juice, or
herbal teas; avoid carbonated
and highly caffeinated drinks that will
hyper-stimulate and stress you further.

Sleep – your brain needs downtime to transfer information from working memory to long-term memory and this occurs during deep and restorative periods of sleep.

Plan – whether this is for a two-day session or a week's marathon, work out what you want to accomplish and chunk it into blocks of work, from preparation to completion.

It always seems impossible until it's done.

NELSON MANDELA

Organising your student finance

It may be the first time you need to organise a financial budget (see page 118-121) but it's well worth getting to grips with this before you embark on student life, especially if you have to juggle a student loan, a grant and limited income.

Work out exactly what you have to live on during term time, what your expenses are, what you need to eat nutritiously – either self-catering or in halls of residence – and what your entertainment/beer money budget might be. If you don't know this, it won't be possible to work out how to make your money last over a period of time. Once you know what your income is, you can break it down into a term-time, monthly, weekly or daily budget, avoiding any shocks, requests for parental help, or expensive loans (on top of student loans). Once you're on top of this, you will then know what any shortfalls might be and whether you will need to find a part-time or holiday job to help finance your student life.

TOP TIP: Check out all student offers that may be available to you – i.e. railcards, free banking, healthcare concessions and student discounts. Research, sign up for and make good use of these: they will save you precious pennies in the long run.

BASIC LIFE SKILLS FOR STUDENTS

Before you embark on life as a student, make sure you know how to:

- Cook a few basic meals – spaghetti bolognese, scrambled eggs, baked potatoes, shepherd's pie, chilli con carne, ratatouille, pasta. Learn how to bulk up more expensive ingredients with cheaper vegetables when you cook.
- Use a washing machine.
- Clean the bathroom (including the toilet!).
- Pay bills.

And finally... organising a student house share

For many students, this might be the first time they share a home – be it a flat, house or other accommodation – with a group of people who are not family, with no parent doing the cleaning up...

Even if everyone has their own study bedroom, communal areas like the kitchen, bathroom and living room need attention. Now you will also find out, probably for the first time too, what different people will tolerate in terms of dirty dishes, taking out the rubbish and cleaning the toilet.

However well meaning everyone plans to be, keeping on top of general household tasks can become an issue and challenge even the most sanguine of us. Better to avoid problems before they start and organise a basic cleaning rota, agreed between you *before* difficulties arise. That way, it's a pragmatic allocation of chores that need to be done, rather than a bone of contention about who does, or doesn't, do what.

Project & event management

Project management could be loosely described as 'getting things organised' and is used in the business world to ensure something is accomplished within a timescale and on budget. It is not necessarily a continuous process, and may depend on delivering finite projects one after another, or concurrently, with one person responsible for the overall management of each.

The definition of a project is that it has a limited timeframe and a defined goal. Understanding this – and clarifying what those two factors are – is the first step. You can then work backwards, identifying each step that needs to be taken along the way.

In terms of general organisation, project management can be a useful model not just in business life but elsewhere, particularly for event planning or organising a family holiday. So, whether you're organising a school trip to the zoo for 30 eight-year-olds, a birthday supper for 12, or a three-day gala for 8,000 participants, many of the key components of your task remain the same.

Six main steps of project management

1. **Define**: what is the aim of the project, what does it need to achieve that and what will the success of the project look like.
2. **Initiate**: what do you need to set up or put in place for the project before you start? Remember, this may involve other people as a resource, too.
3. **Plan**: work out the details of what's necessary to achieve the goal, what resources you have and what the costs might be; delegating roles to other people may also feature here.
4. **Execute**: this is when you do the work identified to deliver the project's goals.
5. **Monitor**: keeping on top of progress, hitting targets, managing other people involved in the project and – if anything goes awry – taking the steps necessary to get things back on track.
6. **Completion**: fulfilling the original goal. This may also include project analysis and feedback.

Every moment and every event of every man's life on earth plants something in his soul.
Thomas Merton, American Trappist monk and writer

Organising an event

When it comes to event planning, identifying the key purpose of the occasion – be it entertainment, celebration, fun or fundraising – influences considerations from location to food to any possible risk assessment.

Here's what a first checklist for an event might look like...
› **Event:** surprise summer picnic for Dad's 50th birthday
› **Theme:** 1970s revival!
› **Date:** Saturday June 20th
› **Where:** the local park (near the boating lake, maps to follow)

> **Invites:** list of 60 people, alert them to the day (& secrecy!) now, invites with details to follow – N.B. copy to printer by beginning of May
> **Food:** ask everyone to bring something to share, specify and co-ordinate nearer the time (N.B. brief on this by June 7th)
> **Drinks:** to provide (+ coolboxes + plastic glasses, N.B. to buy by June 14th)
> **Don't forget:** rugs to sit on, sunscreen and/or cool weather wear, umbrellas (for shade or rain!) – add to information on invite
> **Music:** bring iPod (& make sure it includes 'Happy Birthday To You' by Dad's favourite, Stevie Wonder)

Deciding the date

Once a date is decided upon, you need to let the key players know. This can also mean securing your location of choice, especially if it gets booked up in advance, before sending out invites. Alerting people on your guest list with a 'save the date' request may be a useful exercise, even before other details are available, especially if it's a date that might clash with other people's events or plans.

Location

The type of event you're planning may influence your location, as will the time of year in which you plan to hold it. A winter wedding will need an indoor venue, while a summer picnic can be held in a park – albeit with wet-weather provisos – and a memorial service may need somewhere that's not always available to the public, like a church.

We don't remember days, we remember moments.

CESARE PAVESE, ITALIAN POET, NOVELIST & TRANSLATOR

Numbers

Your location will also influence the numbers you can invite (as will your budget). A child with a winter birthday may need an indoor location, which can restrict numbers, while summer birthdays can be more flexible.

Budget

Once you know your numbers, you can work out a budget – not just for the possible cost of a location, but also for the catering. If you are self-catering you may want to employ some extras to help serve, or go the whole hog with a catered service, which is usually priced per head, so you need to know initial numbers even if these are confirmed at a later date. In any event, event costs can rack up and all aspects – from food to transportation to staffing – can escalate.

Help

What help do you need to realise the event you're organising, and who can help you? This may be family, friends or paid helpers – but they will all need a clear brief from you about their contribution. Delegate different tasks, give them any necessary tools and the timescale required, and keep track of their progress as well as your own.

At the end of the day…

An event should be something to be enjoyed and savoured. Organise it to within an inch of its life… and then let go and enjoy it.

POLAROID

Meetings

When two or more people are gathered together for a specific purpose, you have a meeting. If that purpose is well defined, the meeting should be structured to achieve its aim, be it to organise a company event or plan a family's schedule. Remember, holding meetings should contribute to the process of organisation, rather than distract from it.

Meetings are indispensable when you don't want to do anything. *J. K. Galbraith, American economist and diplomat*

A camel is a horse designed by a committee.

ANON

The purpose of a meeting can include:
› Communicating information
› Brainstorming, sourcing or exchanging ideas
› Progressing work, ways of working and feedback
› Resolving problems and settling disputes
› Taking decisions and agreeing action

Of course, meetings can waste an awful lot of everybody's time, so first make sure a meeting is really necessary and that everyone understands what it is designed to achieve. If you just want to pass on information or ask for feedback, there may be better ways of doing this than having a meeting.

KEY POINTERS OF ANY MEETING
- Keep the numbers of those involved manageable by only including the key people necessary to achieve the meeting's stated purpose.
- Allocate a set amount of time for a meeting. And stick to it.
- Have an agenda for the meeting and make sure its stated aim is known to everyone attending, so that any necessary information-gathering for the meeting is done beforehand.
- Put away all smartphones, tablets, laptops, etc. which could distract those in the meeting. Keeping focused on the meeting while it's in session will make it more efficient.
- Have one person to chair or facilitate the meeting, and another to take notes on what has been agreed upon or actions committed to.

Meetings get a bad rap, and deservedly so – most are disorganised and distracted – but they can be a critical tool for getting your team on the same page. *Justin Rosenstein, co-founder of Asana*

Organising a formal meeting

If you are responsible for organising a more formal meeting, then it's useful to have a checklist of what's expected of you:

> **Location:** do you need to book a room? If so, you need to know the date, time, duration and place of the meeting, plus the number of people you need to accommodate.

> **Invite:** those attending and give them all relevant information about date, location, amount of time needed, etc.

> **Agenda:** you may need to gather information for this, and circulate it with any documentation necessary in good time prior to the meeting.

> **Online:** many meetings now occur online, and when this happens it is as well to have a dummy run with any new technology to check everything is working efficiently before the scheduled time.

> **Follow-up:** this might include circulating minutes and also making sure action agreed is within a timescale.

Organise your digital life

Technology is a good servant but a bad master. Used properly, though, it can help to keep you organised – as long as you keep it organised.

De-clutter your devices

You won't be organised if you can't find anything on your computer, laptop or smartphone, so you will need a basic system for organising files. Keep it simple and use generic folders as you would for an old-fashioned filing cabinet: Admin (Work & Home), Holidays, Finance, etc. Within folders, you can have different files: Tax, Car, Household Bills, etc. Consider your online filing as a virtual filing cabinet. It's no more complicated than that.

Back up and delete

When you're not going to use a file again but can't or don't want to delete it, back it up and archive it to an external hard drive to save space on your computer.

Alternatively, back up your files online. Companies like Google and Apple offer cloud storage, which basically puts your files on to their computers across the internet, and provides a lot of space for free. Go online to see what's available and what might suit your needs.

Don't be a digital hoarder!

Have a regular review of folders that are no longer valid: these can slow down the performance of your computer, laptop or smartphone. Deleting old files will help your organisation, giving you fewer files to sift through, and your computer will also start performing better with less junk and more storage space.

Organise your time for tasks

Make use of your digital calendar and set reminders – that way you'll never forget an important event or anniversary again. You can also use this facility to allocate time for work that you have to do, exercise that you want to fit in, as well as for leisure time – including a reminder to 'do nothing' or go to bed on time!

Organising a workable schedule and sticking with it will also boost your productivity. But be reasonable and don't overdo it, otherwise you may find yourself demotivated if you fail to keep up with the goals you've set yourself.

You will also be able to share key aspects of your working schedule with colleagues via applications like Google Drive, keeping everyone else up to date – not just work colleagues, but family members too.

Keep your emails in check

Emails can easily become overwhelming and an area where, for many people, digital organisation falls down. Endless messages flood our inboxes, so making sure that you see important emails and ignore useless ones can become very difficult.

It can be helpful to have different email addresses: one for work and important correspondence and one you use for shopping, for example.

Once you have given out an email address for anything other than work, you can easily get bombarded by hundreds of marketing emails – but by using a specific address for non-work emails, they won't clog up your inbox and obscure what's important.

Start by unsubscribing to marketing emails you no longer wish to receive. You can do this as they come in, as most have a one-click unsubscribe button on them, usually at the bottom. Alternatively, online software can help do this for you, but this is less secure than routinely doing it yourself.

Divide your emails into folders by labelling addresses and splitting emails up between important work-related messages and those from friends. This makes it easier to identify your email traffic. And use the flag button to keep you aware of emails you've saved and need to reply to.

Apps

Smartphones can help organise our lives. With reminders, timers and calendars, all our activities and needs can be stored and found in one place – all in your pocket – and backed up online by syncing across personal gadgets. But there are other apps that can help you stay organised as well.

Evernote is currently the best note-taking app around. Easy to use and organise, it syncs over an online account, so you can access your notes on all your devices. It's perfect for making notes on the go which you can review at home on your computer.

Google is one provider with many apps to choose from, especially those found on their Google Drive software. Store your files, make new documents and spreadsheets all online and share them with your friends at the click of a button. All you need is a Gmail account to get started.

Any.do is a checklist software that helps you keep track of mini tasks that you need to do. Add them, set deadlines and swipe them away once done. Any.do will keep notifications on your phone to remind you of anything you need to do – as long as you tell it to!

Make sure everything is secure

Online security and privacy are increasingly at risk, so make sure that what you do helps protect you. Documents and folders can be password encrypted with programs like WinZip, and most computers today allow generic computer folders to have password encryptions.

One way to secure your documents is with an online storage provider, like Dropbox, Google Drive or iCloud, where backups are easy to make. Always bear in mind, however, that whatever method you use, it can never be 100 per cent secure as files may still become corrupted or lost.

PREVENT OVEREXPOSURE ONLINE

- Google yourself to see how exposed you are.
- Opt out of any sites that allow 'people search'.
- Set your privacy settings on social networks to the max.
- Avoid using social networking sites like Facebook or Twitter to log on to other sites.
- Never put your full date of birth on any social networking sites.
- Use anonymous web settings and block cookies on your web browser.
- Never share your address book with any website.
- If shopping online, use an alternative email address that you don't use for anything else.

Organise your money

Annual income twenty pounds, annual expenditure nineteen pounds nineteen (shillings) and six (pence), result happiness. Annual income twenty pounds, annual expenditure twenty pounds ought and six, result misery.

Charles Dickens, David Copperfield

Mr Micawber's oft-quoted advice for happiness in Charles Dickens's novel *David Copperfield* may not be quite so relevant today, when debt – from student loans to mortgages to credit cards – is a fact of life rather than a route to the workhouse, but the idea of living within our means still requires some thought. And organising your money is part of that.

From the time we are encouraged as children to save pennies in a piggy bank, to how we use credit as adults, money can be organised to our advantage. Not allowing our outgoings to exceed our income, as Mr Micawber advises, is a first step and can benefit from a monthly budget.

Budget

One key aspect of having a budget is the need to revisit it when life circumstances change. For example, a new job might mean an increased income but also a longer commute, which could increase fixed outgoings. Or you may want to start saving more for a holiday, new car or an event. Buying more, or upgrading possessions, might mean you require more insurance cover.

Even if you only do a rough, back-of-an-envelope calculation of monies going in and out on a monthly basis, it will help work out what you can afford to spend day-to-day. Or use one of the many online budget calculators to do the maths for you, like the one on my website www.moneymagpie.com
Jasmine Birtles

Income – all regular monies coming in from earnings, investments, etc.
Fixed outgoings – rent/mortgage, bills for services (electricity, gas, phone), insurance, credit card repayments, pension pot, etc.
Disposable income – what's left after subtracting outgoings from income.

Having a budget also means you can review where you're spending your money and also, if you need to, where you can make savings. Are you, for example, eating out a lot or relying on takeaways, which are expensive, rather than cooking? Using public transport when you could be walking?

Understanding your relationship to money

Money is never just a means to an end, a tool that enables transactions. Our relationship to money is related to our psychology. It is emotionally loaded, rooted in all sorts of ideas about ourselves – relating to power, security, control, independence, freedom, happiness and so on – which can influence how we organise and manage our money.

WHAT MOTIVATES US?

Psychologists have identified four key ways in which we are motivated by money:

Security – the extent to which money can be used to feel secure and shield us from anxiety about possible future problems.

Power – the extent to which money can be used to wield power and influence over others.

Love – the degree to which money can be used to buy goodwill and affection.

Freedom – the extent to which money can enable the enjoyable things in life.

> **Money is only a tool. It will take you where you wish, but it will not replace you as the driver.** *Ayn Rand*

Online banking

Online access to your bank account makes it easier to organise regular payments, transfer money between accounts and keep track of your spending. Text alerts when you get close to your limit can help avoid unarranged (and therefore costly) overdraft payments.

Money management apps

If you are into gadgets, there are numerous apps that can help you organise and manage your money, and many are free. Goodbudget will create a budget based on cash flow; BillGuard syncs with your bank account, protects against fraud and helps you understand your spending habits; and HomeBudget provides clear, colour-coded categories for Expenses, Bills, Income, Budget and Accounts.

If we command our wealth, we shall be rich and free. If our wealth commands us, we are poor indeed.

EDMUND BURKE

Shop around

Financial markets constantly change, so it's always worth checking out whether you can save money on utility bills, bank charges, mortgage rates, mobile phone tariffs and insurance premiums. It takes a bit of time to check the small print, but it really does pay to check out the deals regularly and many comparison websites exist to make this easier.

Often, financial offers only favour new customers: strangely, the best deals are seldom offered for loyalty! But always ask, as often you can personally negotiate a better deal.

Avoid late payment charges

Many utility companies actually reward you for paying on time – and this is easy to do if your regular payments are automated – while paying late can sometimes incur financial penalties, which can add up over time. Missing payments or paying them late will also affect your credit rating.

Avoid bank charges

Again, this is money wasted. The only fail-safe way to completely avoid bank charges is to keep in credit at all times. That's not always easy, of course, but it's the 'unarranged overdraft' that is so expensive, racking up daily charges plus interest. Some banks provide the immediate facility of an interest-free overdraft to a specified limit, for occasional mismatches between income and outgoings. This should only be used as a potential cushion, not a regular occurrence.

TOP TIP: Saving money regularly, however small the amount, is easier if you think of it as a deduction from your fixed outgoings rather than as an optional extra from your disposable income.

Debt

Debt (especially credit card debt) is expensive because the interest rates are so high. The smart way to use credit cards is to pay them off every month, so that your credit usage is only over a few weeks and free. Generally speaking, if you need to incur debt, find the cheapest option. For example, those with mortgages might find it easier to borrow against that, rather than take out a short-term loan at expensive rates.

Credit rating

As soon as you start to be active with your money – for example, with a first bank account, bills in your name, or as a student with a loan – your 'credit rating' starts to exist. A credit rating is based on your ability to pay back debt and the likelihood of defaulting on a debt. Effectively, every bill is a debt, so if you are late, miss a payment or fail to pay it, this scores against your credit rating. Building a good credit rating is important because it will allow you to have a credit card, mortgage or other forms of borrowing and, usually, the better your credit rating, the more competitive an interest rate.

TOP TIPS TO IMPROVE CREDIT RATING

- Always, *always* pay bills on time – use automated payments where you can.
- Use a credit card to build credit scores but always pay monthly, even if it's only the minimum amount, and pay off the full amount whenever you can.
- Never use a credit card for cash withdrawals or payday loans, as this shows poor money management and incurs immediate interest charges.
- Avoid continuously applying for credit, as it shows up on credit checks and reduces your credit rating.
- Being on the electoral roll provides evidence of stability through where you live.

Check your credit record with an online facility like Experian or Equifax, and if there's anything affecting it badly that is not your fault – perhaps a previous tenant at the same address had defaulted on a debt and this is affecting you – query it in writing and get it removed.
Jasmine Birtles, www.moneymagpie.com

Never spend your money before you have it.

THOMAS JEFFERSON

Organise your holidays

A report commissioned by Teletext Holidays in 2014 found that holiday makers spent more time planning and organising their holiday than actually enjoying it.

Which is a shame, given how precious is time away from work spent with our families. The Teletext research showed an average of 13 hours spent researching accommodation and 11 hours sorting out the travel arrangements – so a lot of time is spent getting organised, and this doesn't include the immediate preparation of packing.

All in all, going on holiday can make the most stalwart of travellers anxious. So how can being organised help avoid pre-holiday tension and ensure that time spent away is relaxing and restorative?

Take a rest: a field that is rested gives a beautiful crop. *Ovid*

First steps

Decide on a budget and break your holiday organisation down into three distinct components:

› **Destination:** bear in mind travel distance, climate conditions at the time of travel, and the specific needs of yourself and your holiday companions – for example, young children might struggle in the heat.
› **Travel:** this may involve a sequence of flights, train bookings, taxis, buses and car journeys. Bear in mind options about time and cost and what suits all those travelling: for some, getting to the airport at 5 a.m. is no problem, while for others it's a logistical no-no.
› **What will be needed for travel:** passports, visas, medical requirements like vaccinations – some of which need forward planning.

Air travel

Every airline has its own security protocols and these can include the size of what can be carried on as hand luggage. Check the small print online as it will be you who is inconvenienced if you try to bend the rules at check-in.

Budget airlines are great for students and anyone who is happy to travel with just a rucksack and a toothbrush, using the plane like a bus, but for those who prefer a little more in terms of seat allocation and customer service, be prepared to pay for it.

Pack any essentials in your hand luggage, in case your main luggage goes astray and fails to make it to your destination. And don't forget your travel survival kit, including toothbrush and toothpaste, wipes, moisturiser for long-haul flights, and any medication you may need for the duration of travel.

TOP TIP: Scan a copy of your passport and any other important documentation and send this to yourself as an email attachment that can be accessed while abroad. In the case of lost or stolen documentation, it may be useful to have access to the details you need for consular help. This can also be particularly useful for the parents of young people travelling alone – should the worst happen and they need to sort it out, they – and you! – will have access to full details.

TRAVEL CHECKLIST

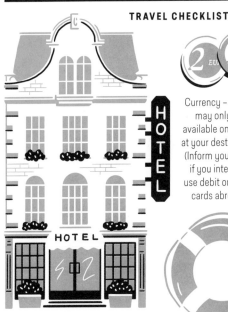

Currency – which may only be available on arrival at your destination. (Inform your bank if you intend to use debit or credit cards abroad).

Passport AND (if required) visa.

Travel insurance – covering medical care, repatriation, lost or stolen items and legal cover.

Accommodation confirmation (this may also need printing off).

Travel tickets – this may include flight check-in online and printed-off boarding passes.

Other transport bookings, including car hire documentation and your driving licence.

Vacation – a period of travel and relaxation when you take twice the clothes and half the money you need.

ANON

Travel itinerary

If your holiday involves several locations, or if you have a number of excursions planned and booked, remove any stress by creating an itinerary that lists key facts like departure times and contact numbers, day by day, so that you have a quick checklist – and one that can be shared, if necessary, among fellow travellers.

Bear in mind that if you have your itinerary on an electronic gadget, rather than in printed-off form, an absence of power supply could restrict your access to the details you need, when you need them.

Packing

First considerations when organising your packing for a trip are:

› Weather at destination – and what time you arrive: it can be quite chilly at 3 a.m. even in a tropical climate.
› Length of stay – although you won't need much more for a four-week holiday than a week-long one.

> Any specific activities – e.g. swimming, skiing, walking, or a formal social event. Before loading everything into your case, lay out your chosen items in organised piles. This will help with the planning, and also prevent you having to take things in and out of your bag to check what you have or haven't included. Decide what you are going to wear to travel in before you pack, and keep these clothes to one side. (Make sure you don't duplicate those items you are travelling in.)

> Place shoes and heavy items at what will be the bottom of your case when upright.

> Decant liquids into smaller, plastic, securely stoppered containers and wrap inside a plastic bag.

> If your holiday destination supplies bath and beach towels, it's still worth packing a cotton sarong or hammam (traditional Turkish) towel, which packs flat and can double as a beach wrap, towel or even picnic cloth.

> Never pack in a suitcase anything valuable that you wouldn't want to lose.

> Remember that you can hand-wash underwear or use a laundry service for clothes when you're away, which helps cut down on taking too many duplicate items.

TOP TIP: If a child is holidaying without you, and you want them to return with all their belongings, then ensure they pack with you and include a checklist of items taken, so they can check on this when they are packing to return home. This will also help them learn to become more self-reliant and responsible for their own possessions.

Finally...

In an ideal world, going on holiday would mean leaving our work life at home... but the reality is that few of us travel anywhere without at least a mobile or smartphone. We have become increasingly reliant on our electronic gadgets – from iPads to digital cameras – so remember to take any chargers you need, and relevant travel plugs or adapters for your holiday destination.

On vacation, you can wear all the colourful and casual clothing that you like, but you must always be elegant.

CHRISTIAN DIOR

Done & dusted

There are a hundred and one reasons not to get organised, but only one reason to do so: it will make your life easier.

It's true. Getting all your ducks in a row is easier if you're organised. Wasting time looking for lost items, buying more stuff you don't need, creating problems you can't solve – they all make life more difficult than it needs to be.

Getting organised may feel like it's a means to an end, but it's also an end in itself. What's more, it can be done incrementally, bit by bit, over time, which is why this book focuses on different aspects of life and how you might benefit from the organisation of each area.

The secret of getting ahead is getting started. The secret of getting started is breaking your complex overwhelming tasks into small manageable tasks, and then starting on the first one. *Mark Twain*

The ultimate goal is to organise life so that it can be lived in a more efficient, de-cluttered and stress-free way. And that gives you more time to do what you want, rather than what you don't.

Clear your stuff. Clear your mind.

ERIC M. RIDDLE, AUTHOR OF *STUFFOLOGY 101*

Acknowledgements

Thanks are due to my editor Kajal Mistry for all her cheerful help and attention to detail, and who ensured I stayed organised on this book; and to Julia Murray whose talented design and illustrations bring life to its pages. Thanks, too, to my publisher Kate Pollard and the rest of the team at Hardie Grant, whose enthusiastic commitment to this new book in the series made it happen.

And, finally, in acknowledgement of my two children, Josh and Robbie: whose impact on my life also taught me that being organised made life much simpler in the long run.

Appendix

Further reading

Minimalism: Live a meaningful life,
Joshua Fields Millburn and Ryan Nicodemus, Asymmetrical Press

Mrs Beeton's Book of Household Management,
Isabella Beeton, Oxford Paperbacks (abridged edition)

Stuffocation: Living more with less,
James Wallman, Penguin

The Life-Changing Magic of Tidying,
Marie Kondo, Vermilion

The 7 Habits of Highly Effective People,
Stephen R. Covey, Simon & Schuster

Useful apps

Any.do / BillGuard / Evernote / Goodbudget
/ Google Drive / HomeBudget

About the author

Harriet Griffey is a journalist, writer and author
of numerous books focused on health. Along with
I Want to Be Calm and *I Want to Sleep,* published
by Hardie Grant, she is also the author of *The Art of
Concentration*, *How to Get Pregnant* and *Give Your
Child a Better Start* (with Professor Mike Howe) and
writes regularly on health-related and other issues for
the national press. She originally trained as a nurse
and is also an accredited coach with Youth at Risk
(www.youthatrisk.org.uk).

Index

I Want to Be Organised by Harriet Griffey

First published in 2016 by Hardie Grant Books

Hardie Grant Books (UK)
5th & 6th Floors
52–54 Southwark Street
London SE1 1UN
www.hardiegrant.co.uk

Hardie Grant Books (Australia)
Ground Floor, Building 1
658 Church Street
Melbourne, VIC 3121
www.hardiegrant.com.au

British Library Cataloguing-in-Publication Data. A catalogue record
for this book is available from the British Library.

ISBN: 978-1-78488-024-8

Publisher: Kate Pollard
Senior Editor: Kajal Mistry
Editorial Assistant: Hannah Roberts
Internal and Cover Design: Julia Murray
Internal and Cover Illustrations: Julia Murray
Copy Editor: Zelda Turner
Proofreader: Lorraine Jerram
Indexer: Cathy Heath
Colour Reproduction by p2d

Printed and bound in China by 1010

10 9 8 7 6 5 4 3 2 1